WITHDRAWN
Anne Arundel Co. Public Library

TRUCK DRIVERS

CHRISTINE HONDERS

PowerKiDS press™

New York

Published in 2020 by The Rosen Publishing Group, Inc.
29 East 21st Street, New York, NY 10010

Copyright © 2020 by The Rosen Publishing Group, Inc.

All rights reserved. No part of this book may be reproduced in any form without permission in writing from the publisher, except by a reviewer.

First Edition

Editor: Greg Roza
Book Design: Reann Nye

Photo Credits: Cover, p.1 Ariel Skelley/DigitalVision/Getty Images; pp. 4–22 Abstractor/Shutterstock.com; p. 5 Vitpho/Shutterstock.com; p. 7 rCarner/Shutterstock.com; p. 9 Natalia Bratslavsky/Shutterstock.com; p. 11 gk-6mt/iStock/Getty Images Plus/Getty Images; p. 13 Everett Media/Shutterstock.com; p. 15 Mindscape studio/Shutterstock.com; pp. 17, 19 kali9/E+/Getty Imgaes; p. 21 IM_photo/Shutterstock.com; p. 22 Colorblind Images LLC/DigitalVision/Getty Images.

Library of Congress Cataloging-in-Publication Data

Names: Honders, Christine, author.
Title: Truck drivers / Christine Honders.
Description: New York : PowerKids Press, 2020. | Series: Helpers in our
  community | Includes index.
Identifiers: LCCN 2019016084| ISBN 9781725308305 (pbk.) | ISBN 9781725308329
  (library bound) | ISBN 9781725308312 (6 pack)
Subjects: LCSH: Truck drivers–Juvenile literature. | Trucking–Juvenile
  literature.
Classification: LCC HD8039.M795 H66 2020 | DDC 388.3/24023–dc23
LC record available at https://lccn.loc.gov/2019016084

Manufactured in the United States of America

CPSIA Compliance Information: Batch #CWPK20. For Further Information contact Rosen Publishing, New York, New York at 1-800-237-9932.

CONTENTS

A World Without Trucks

We've all seen trucks on the road. What would happen if they were gone? In three days, grocery stores would be empty. Bottled water would be gone in two weeks. Bank machines would be empty in just two days! That's why we need truck drivers.

What Truck Drivers Do

Factories produce things we use every day. Farmers grow food for millions of people. Truck drivers **transport** these goods across the country. They drive thousands of miles and take them to stores. Then people can buy what they need.

Tractor Trailers

Many truck drivers use tractor trailers. A tractor trailer is a large truck with two parts hooked together. The front part is the truck. The back part is the trailer, which is a huge box on wheels. These boxes can carry many different things—including cars and toys!

Driving on 18 Wheels

Driving a big truck isn't the same as driving a car. Tractor trailers have 18 wheels and can weigh 35,000 pounds (15,876 kg)! It's much harder to control one. Truck drivers get special training. They practice driving with loads of **cargo**. They learn to drive safely with other **vehicles** on the road.

STUDENT
DRIVER

Flatbed Trucks

Not everything fits into a tractor trailer. Flatbed trucks transport large, weirdly shaped items from place to place. They carry wood, metal, and heavy machines to **construction** sites. They carry plows to farmers. Flatbed drivers even carry airplane parts and big tanks!

OVERSIZE LOAD

13

Tanker Trucks

Tanker truck drivers transport **liquids**. Some liquids, such as milk or water, are harmless. Other tankers carry **hazardous** liquids. Many transport oil, gas, or **chemicals** that can start a fire. If something happens to a tanker truck, the driver and other people on the road could be hurt.

Rolling Refrigerators

Some people drive refrigerated trucks. They carry foods, such as meat and ice cream, that must stay cold. Some drugs must be kept cold, too. Refrigerated trucks bring these medicines to hospitals that need them. Truck drivers help save lives!

Workplace on Wheels

Truck drivers spend up to 11 hours a day in their trucks. They work weekends and holidays. They drive all night long to bring people their goods on time. Some truck drivers have beds in their trucks! They take naps if they're too sleepy to drive.

Lonely Job

Truck drivers have a lonely job. Some drivers are on the road for weeks. They spend hours by themselves with no one to talk to. Truck drivers give up time with their families to bring our families what they need.

We Need Truck Drivers!

Truck drivers transport food to stores. They transport the things needed to build homes and roads. They transport gas for our cars and medicine to keep us healthy. Some even transport live animals! Truck drivers work very hard to keep our communities growing!

GLOSSARY

cargo: Goods carried by a plane, train, or truck.

chemical: Matter that can be mixed with other matter to cause changes.

construction: Having to do with the act of building something.

hazardous: Dangerous, or not safe.

liquid: Something that's able to flow freely, such as water.

transport: To carry something from one place to another.

vehicle: A machine used to carry people or goods from one place to another.

INDEX

WEBSITES

Due to the changing nature of Internet links, PowerKids Press has developed an online list of websites related to the subject of this book. This site is updated regularly. Please use this link to access the list: www.powerkidslinks.com/HIOC/truckdrivers